Animal
Life

Also by Mario Milosevic

Novels
Claypot Dreamstance
The Coma Monologues
The Doctor and the Clown
Kyle's War
The Last Giant
Splitting
Terrastina and Mazolli

Collections
15 Strange Tales of Crime and Mystery
Entangled Realities (with Kim Antieau)
Labor Days
Miniatures

Poetry
Fantasy Life
Love Life

Animal Life

poems by Mario Milosevic

Animal Life
by Mario Milosevic

Copyright © 2004 by Mario Milosevic

ISBN-13: 978-1-949644-13-5

No part of this book may be reproduced without written permission of the author.

Published by Green Snake Publishing
www.greensnakepublishing.com

for Agica

Contents

- 11 Food Chain
- 12 When I Was
- 14 Stilled Heart
- 15 My Tattoo
- 16 On Learning That Owls Hunt by Starlight
- 17 Evidence
- 18 Patricide, Parasites, and Pesticides
- 19 Leaving
- 20 A Disturbance in the Field
- 21 A Falls Creek Morning
- 22 Kinship
- 23 The Snake Fear
- 24 Dinner and Dancing
- 25 Destinies
- 26 Roadkill
- 27 Hold Still Please
- 28 Food and Sex on the Grounds Surrounding Maryhill Museum
- 29 The Age of Faith
- 30 A Totem's Work is Never Done
- 31 Slow Footsteps Protect Tiny Lives
- 32 Reindeer Presence
- 33 Passing a Dog and its Owner on the Trail to Hamilton Mountain
- 34 Theory and Practice

35	Bird Brains
36	White Pigeons White Bones White Moon
37	Osprey
38	An Afternoon in Paradise
39	He Breaks Their Necks
40	Midnight Enlightenment
41	The Beak
42	Land Development
43	Planted
44	Nothing Lasts Forever
45	Frequent Flyer
46	She's Eve: A Walking Poem
47	Before Experimenting on Certain Animals it is Always Advisable…
48	The Birds
50	What a Friend Told Me About the Men in Her Family
51	It's Like a Reflection of Life
52	The Power of Myth
53	The Pond on a Day Without Wind
54	Elk
55	Our Cat, Who Used to Bring Live Snakes Into the House
56	René Descartes Looked Through a Bull's Eyeball
57	The Sad Vegetarian
58	Canine Reminder
59	Yip Yip Yip
60	Scavengers
61	The Sound of Blue Jays at 6 a.m.

62	An Ode to Moles
63	Lunch Break
64	Calling Card
65	Milk
66	Last Rites for Roadkill
67	Menagerie
68	Frying Eggs
69	Cycle of Metamorphosis
70	There's a Yellow Ladybug
71	Comfort Zone
72	Location Location Location
73	Juncos
74	Sanderling Flight, Sanderling Walk
75	Final Journey
76	Lost and Found
77	Missing Fingers
78	An Insomniac's Machinations
79	Evolutionary Thoughts
80	In Ancient Times We Crawled Around On Our Bellies and Did...
81	Unnatural Selection
82	Deep Time
83	Being Content With Who You Are
84	Not Much of a Protector
86	Suddenly Dangerous
87	Spring Morning After the Last Snow Has Melted

- 88   Bigfoot
- 89   Perfectionism
- 90   Rudderless in Bandon
- 91   Still Healthy
- 92   Shadows Make the Ground More Real
- 93   Alzheimer's
- 94   Genealogy
- 100 The Index to the Bestiary of Extinct Species
- 101 Plato's Menagerie

- 102 Dramatis Personae
- 103 Acknowledgements
- 104 About the Author

Food Chain

Once I met a man who thought
he knew the future. He said,
nature is eating or being eaten.
There's nothing in between so
I know tomorrow I'm going to
eat or I'm going to be eaten. It's
the same with these animals. In
the wild they have to hunt or be
hunted. He said this while we
were at a zoo, standing in front
of a leopard who languished at
the top of a wooden catwalk,
regarding us through iron bars
with cold eyes but with tail
still flicking. The man was
talking to his son, who was no
more than eight, licking an ice
cream cone and taking in those
eyes. I watched the man place
a hand on the top part of his
son's back and ease him away
from the front of the leopard
cage. As the man passed by me
I saw his eyes were rimmed
with pink. I looked at the leopard
but did not see what had passed
between her and the man. She
held her secret while I stared as
long as the zoo keepers let me.
Then they said we'll be closing
soon sir time to go home.

When I Was

When I was a bear
I filled the world.
My paws were wide,
and I walked large.
I ate all summer
and slept all winter,
dreaming of the time

when I was a dragonfly
and I wove the world.
Darting through air,
skimming over grass,
hovering on water,
my compound eyes
embroidering my dreams of the time

when I was a turtle
and I carried the world.
Walking slowly with the weight,
squat body on four thick legs,
hard shell holding me in,
keeping my dreams of the time

when I was a salmon
and I fed the world.
Sleek skin sliding down river throats,
pink flesh nourishing my cousins.
I swam upstream,
where death took me
and I swallowed my dreams of the time

when I was a tree
and I held the world.
Roots gripping soil,
branches embracing sky,
my vision
encompassing dreams of the time

when I was a raven
and I sang the world.
Single note struck from my throat,
pushed into air,
the sound a call to listen
to the unseen
and honor my dreams of the time

when I was a bear;
when I was a dragonfly;
when I was a turtle, a salmon, a tree;
when I was a raven.

Stilled Heart

They pull the cover
from the bird cage.

Inside the steel ribs
a clump of silent feathers

fallen to a tiny heap.
Light means nothing

now, no animation, and
a feeling of shame seeing

the interior like looking
through a keyhole.

The cloth slips to the
floor, muffled echoes of

beating wings, crumples
wrinkling the cold air.

My Tattoo

lives like a snake,
curled around my imagination,

flicking tongue touching
my skin where the needles

will bite and draw blood
repeatedly to stain my pale

canvas and make a home for
a shedder of skin, twisting

dry scales like tiny shingles
on a house too small to build.

On Learning that Owls Hunt by Starlight

She had a broken wing
and one useless eye,
the work of a windshield
traveling at sixty miles per hour.
She earned her food
by perching quietly for visitors
at the High Desert Museum,
talons wrapped around a dowel,
her keeper explaining
how she used to live.

She hunted at night,
no moon necessary.
The paltry photons
from balls of gas light years away
were sufficient to alert her
to the motions of furry creatures
scrabbling on the desert floor.

I thought about those
mice and chipmunks,
betrayed by the by-products
of distant nuclear reactions.
But mostly I wondered
about the windshield,
cutting down the owl in mid flight.
Did it sustain damage?
Did it carry a starry imprint of the owl's impact?

Evidence

feather tinged with red
bits of bone and skin
obscured tracks in nearby dust

a moment of silence
trying to identify
the meal and the diner

Patricide,
Parasites,
and Pesticides

When the world
comes at you
like a crazy dog,
offer it a biscuit
made of indifference.
It'll trot away to
gnaw on the treat
while you tiptoe
to the cave entrance.
And find refuge
in the darkness,
dripping like stale water
pulling open the tear
in your notions of reality.

Leaving

In the dream
a red-winged blackbird
builds a nest
using tufts of my hair
slices of my skin
and crumbs of my bone
all stuck together
with drops of my blood.

My eyes see
eggs in the nest
that hatch
into greedy little mouths
that get stuffed
with chunks of flesh
pulled from my body.

The hatchlings grow
and fly away
and the nest
made from my body
begins to rot
in the sun and rain.

I reach for it
but my skeletal
half gone hand
is useless.

All I can do is watch
as my heat slips away
and I think only
of those red-winged
blackbirds
soaring above me
fueled by my protein
following my dream.

A Disturbance in the Field

When the lake
in front of my house
shrinks to a shallow pool
surrounded by wet mud,
the great blue heron
that solitary wader
comes looking for fish.
Sitting on my couch
from a quarter mile away
I watch her
through binoculars.
She steps
deliberately.
Her beak flashes,
enters the water,
comes out with a
wriggling meal.
The train passes
and sounds its
harsh whistles
hurting my ear.
The heron maintains
her steady composure
stepping stepping
looking for her next course.
I open the front door
step outside.
The heron cranks
squawks at the sound
of my presence
flies to some place
less oppressive.

A Falls Creek Morning

Pillar of wet sound
flowing white and
holding up the sky.
Mist filling the air
like floating dander
brightened by sunlight.
We stand on the mossed
ejecta of a long dead
volcano and watch
butterflies rest their
wings before returning
to the cool air.

Kinship

Broken insects
writhing on the ground
teach us language
is as universal
as whimpering dogs
flopping fish
and twitching birds.
They all share
the same grammar
and syntax of pain
and make us alive
to the need
to help our
fellow creatures
live past
their story of
agony
or end it
with a final
euthanasiac
period.

The Snake Fear

No limbs or maybe just one.
Made of it, a creature
built like a rubber arm
with no elbow but curving
at infinite bendings. Their
unblinking eyes and that
tiny tongue always flickering
at air. Sometimes if you skin
them, even after they're dead,
they will shudder and pulse
and writhe. A hot pillar of
flickering life in your hands.
Your head fills with blood,
the shed skin wet and crumpled,
touching the dusty ground.
Waiting for the motion to stop.
Around you the beating in your
ears. Tiny slithers up your back.

Dinner and Dancing

The spider spins a web with glee,
Which traps bugs like a flea or bee.
This prompts a spider eating spree,
And thus she gets her calorie.
Such fare would sicken thee or me,
But she can't stand our tea or brie,
And healthy salads make her flee.
But after insect meals you'll see
How merrily she bends her knee,
Dancing her web with spirit free,
Strumming the strands of filigree,
In arachnid eight part harmony.

Destinies

The turtle egg on the path to the cow pasture,
the shell unwound like a white ribbon,
the yolk a yellow smear against the black gravel.
When it was still soft a scavenger must have dug it up
and wrecked it, trying to get at some small bit of
sustenance. I have seen the turtles in the hot afternoon
sun, digging with their hind legs, muddying the ground,
loosening it up, making it nursery suitable. I know they
do not nurture their eggs once they have planted them
in the soil. They return to the pond and will never know,
as I now know, what happened to one of their offspring.

Roadkill

I've heard a good
rule of thumb
is if the flies

haven't gotten
to it yet
then it's ok

to eat. I've
never tested
the theory and

don't expect to
any time soon.
The tires keep

serving them up
like rubber
spatulas pressing

out the juices.
And other tires
come along and

make a relief
painting of them.
Sometimes I'll

study the glyph
the blood paints
on the road. It's

like a highway
gallery. Look for
meaning. Maybe a

sign from beyond
the other lane.
On the other side

Hold Still Please

My first look through a microscope:
frenzy of tiny balloon cells
translucent with jelly organs
and waving cilia
all trembling and shuffling
and eating and pursuing
their puffed up neighbors
while oblivious to the big eye
above them looking down.

How odd it was
that I could see these things
too small for my unaided vision
and too frantic for my slow pencil
scratchy graphite path
trying to capture their portraits.

Food and Sex on the Grounds Surrounding Maryhill Museum

High above the Columbia River
this oasis of peacock habitat
has been carved green from
the surrounding yellow desert.

We eat our lunch at one of
the picnic tables in the shadow
of planted orange trees and before
long those necks come thrusting

toward us, bending like snakes
tipped with beak tongues, the
flock of them: peahens and
peacocks tamed by easy food.

We break off chunks of sandwiches,
toss bits of bread and lettuce
to them, some fruit, a few chips.
We are doing our part to subvert

natural selection and are amused,
for a short time, by their frenzy
of fighting over a crumb or two.
One of the peacocks stands away

from the unruly banquet. He fans
his iridescent feathers in an arc
of dazzling color and struts his
trembling desire, ignoring other

hungers, wanting to catch a hen's
unseeing gaze, while she, intent on
a bouncing apple core, benefits by
his thinning of the day's food chain.

The Age of Faith

Who knows what worlds
crowd the egg safely
colded in my fridge?

Like the thoughts
flitting through the skull
in the car hurtling past me
in the other lane
these are vapors
keeping me alive.

And the knowledge
grown from ignorance
of the matings
will not snap apart
in the hot field of awareness.

There is love surely
in the understanding
that what lies behind
the opaque screens
is a reason for making
people laugh.

The one who jokes
wants the others to laugh:
Like an insect
intent on the center
of a flower
knowing how to extract
what it does not
even know is there.

A Totem's Work is Never Done

the turquoise bear
shiny guardian
a carved salmon
in its mouth

familiar talisman
on the car dashboard
sheltered by a sky blue
windshield's tint

tiny eyes
sunk in stone
watching for hazards
waiting forever
to finish her meal

Slow Footsteps Protect Tiny Lives

Oh, to be a mouse,
rooting among the giants,
sheltered by their loose quilts
of green waves.

The trees stand still
for we little creatures,
who briefly scratch at their feet,
relieving an itch, perhaps,
before flitting away
in a light flash
recorded in their
slow accumulation
of fleshy rings.

Reindeer Presence

Some say you pull Santa's sled
across the dark expanse.
But you are the true shamans
of the north, pulling our spirits
behind you across the frigid plains.
We follow your clicking heels,
your hot breath clouding
the sky and leading the way.
We see your antlers sprout
and fall each season,
like the northern sun,
every rising and setting
marking half a year.
Reindeer, you are keepers of time,
your souls always moving.
You eat lichen and moss,
swallowing the magic of the Earth.
You know nothing of us
but we see your other-worldly ways,
and we know your wild heart
is the only gift we ever need.

Passing a Dog and its Owner on the Trail to Hamilton Mountain

Tongue like a
flesh waterfall
flowing over the rocks
of its teeth.
Taut leash anchored
at its neck
and straightening
its owner's arm,
pointing at the path
they are following.

It's a family I'm seeing.
Alpha hound running the show.
Omega human tagging along
for the ride.

I raise my eyebrows
and nod as we pass.
The taller of the two
feigns a kind of control
of the situation
and nods so slightly
as to seem a tiny shiver.

Theory and Practice

Ever wonder how a particle
can affect another particle
that's millions of light years
away? asks the rogue physicist.

I think it's because there is
only one particle and only one
infinitesimal instant of time.
And what we see all around us,
the profusion of matter,
and the absurd bounty of time,
all of this is not real.
It's all just infinitely repeated
images of those proto bits of space-time.
It's like putting a mirror in front
of a mirror and creating reflections
that go on forever.

I nod as I listen to the physicist.
Interesting, I say, as I look
through the window behind him
and see a black crow strutting
around the caterpillar tracks
of a yellow back hoe, head tilted,
beak thrust to the sky. Later
the operator will climb into the cab
and animate the back hoe's scoop.
He will pull up dirt and pile it into
a dump truck. The crow will have
flown away and I will remember its
quizzical stance long after
I will have forgotten
the crazy physicist and his silly mirrors.

Bird Brains

Modestly proportioned,
they're big enough
to coordinate flight paths,
navigate lofty migrations, and
perform great swooping arcs
that our oversized skulls
can only dream about
and envy.

White Pigeons
White Bones
White Moon

Not the distant flying points
but the flock you see
cutting circles in the air

making you think of doves
for a brief peace but then
hallucinating them into

a fluid skeleton stitched
by invisible ligaments
holding a roundness shaping

a flying moon free of Earth's
hold and casting fleeting
shadows on the eclipsed hill

where a vast ghost face
unfurls gray ribbons fraying
over grass seeing the birds

as bones and chattering a name
in ragged stuttering syllables
hiccupping an endless fugue.

Osprey

You sit on the deck and tell me
your troubles, how you
can't seem to decide what
to do about them, how the
need to sustain yourself
conflicts with the need to
live easy in a world that does
not know who you are.

Behind you, over the lake, an
osprey hovers with wings
paddling the air in short
quick graceless strokes for
a few seconds, then dives,
dropping like a stone,
splashing like bickering spouses
shredding the silence.

But the osprey
pulls out of the water,
its talons embedded
in a silver fish,
hanging like a rudder
as it sails to the top
of a tree to dig in.

I nod as you speak
and I tend to the salmon
grilling on the barbecue,
and offer you a big piece
when it is ready. But
you politely refuse such a
large portion and after the meal
I wrap some up for you
in silver foil to take home
as you say thank you
for a wonderful time.

An Afternoon in Paradise

Goose shit on the trail
means there aren't enough
predators here. No wolverines
or badgers raiding nests
for those succulent eggs.
They all hatch into goslings
and eat and eat and grow until
they make eggs of their own.
Nature's way, so we've been
told. Around me the beauty
of the gorge, also nature's
way, remains unseen by me.
I'm intent on not stepping
on these goose droppings.
They draw my vision down
to where my feet, dodging
like a punch drunk boxer
weaving, navigates this
multiuse obstacles course.
We're all made of something
and we all just want to see
something beyond the now.

He Breaks Their Necks

If you really want someone to blame,
start with that Shakespearean scholar
who decided all the birds mentioned in Will's plays
should be imported to North America.

He brought several species to Central Park
that had no business being there,
including the aggressive European starling
which soon developed expansionist ambitions.

Starlings quickly spread over the continent,
attacking the hatchlings of other species,
hurling them to the ground, and taking
up residence in their nests and bird houses.

A hundred years later in Oregon's Willamette Valley
we tour a place called Bird Haven that nurtures
thousands of mosquito-eating swallows and has to deal
with the descendants of those imported starlings.

The owner explains how he traps them
in his specially designed starling trap and then pauses
as we smile nervously and breathe once, twice,
until someone asks What do you do with them then?

He puts his fists together lightly
and pantomimes a quick little twist
like he's snapping a carrot in two and someone says
Oh, oh, I could never do that.

He shrugs and says another visitor
once told him about her method for starling control.
She puts her trapped birds into plastic bags
and leaves them in the sun for a few hours.

She could not make herself break bird necks and
all I can think is what suffering because centuries ago
some playwright spelled out the word starling
on a piece of paper with the ink-soaked tip of a bird's feather.

Midnight Enlightenment

Spoon laden with honey
dripping amber threads
onto the split bagel.
The darkness outside
keeps its distance
from my kitchen light.
I thank the blessed bees
for their part
in bringing the sun
to my after hours repast.
Bright taste of nectar
filling my mouth
with sweet illumination.

The Beak

the beak tapping
on the eaves

sound of it
flying into the house

I think I hear
mice in the walls

a spider traversing
the ceiling stops

quiet persistence
in the tapping

a thrusting after bits
of blown grain

this house
intercepts the wind

feathered logic
finds the meal

leaves no
footprints

finds
no rest

Land Development

Around the corner the blackberries
have claimed a lot where a house
still stands, only the chimney visible
above the riot of green vines.
Raccoons live there now,
imported like the blackberry bushes,
making a wild home in our neighborhood.
I've seen families of them,
Mom and Dad, three little ones
trailing behind like fat beads
on a string, the row of them
tunneling into their forest,
ignoring the thorns, tasting
the juice, perhaps, waiting for
darkness to return. Poised to move
through a nocturnal existence,
where they are more than visitors.

Planted

She stands in the woods, an open star,
like a gardener recklessly offering
great heaps of bounty to neighbors
and strangers and even the clutch

of blackbirds waiting impatiently
in a nearby tree for their chance
to taste the red flesh of strawberry
weights drooping toward the ground.

Nothing Lasts Forever

The woodpecker
outside my window
tat tat tatting
for bugs does not
know how
the sound keeps
me from the
important task
of maintaining
a connection with
the natural world
by meditating
in a calm quiet space.
I will the bird to
find a nice juicy
grub to take back
to its nest. Then
all is silent as I
sit peacefully and
contemplate the
tree and prepare
to clear my mind
just as the woodpecker
returns for seconds.

Frequent Flyer

They're messing with the templates.
Putting grasshopper genes
into eggplants or committing
some equivalent insanity.

Someone's going to patent
my genes one of these days.
It may as well be me.

Don't they have a form for that?
What do I do? Scrape off a few
skin cells and slip them into
an envelope and mail them to
the patent office?

In the meantime, what do
I make for dinner? The eggplant
keeps jumping off the counter
to the kitchen floor.

The stove is
flyover country now and
the grasshopper's ancient escaping
stratagem is part of my dinner.

What if the clerk at the patent
office can't read my dna?
What if someone sends in my dna first?
Could someone build me
from a few shed cells?

Who will hear the roar?
From over my way
none of it will matter
like it once did.
A unique identity
will be a weakened concept
fit only for nostalgia.
They'll call it a luxury
we can't afford anymore.

She's Eve: A Walking Poem

Shrouded in black
she hops after
the dark seeds
encased in apple flesh.

She stands and caws,
one foot gripping
apple skin.
Her beak pokes,
brings up
a sweet offering.

Awkward effort
to retrieve
the pebbles
at the core.
Black tear drops
she has never shed.

Before Experimenting on Certain Animals it is Always Advisable to Disable Their Vocal Chords

Because you can't turn off your ears.
No arguments now.
The chords can be cut humanely
and though you may be haunted
by the subsequent silent screams
you can always pretend
it is someone else performing
the cutting and the burning.
The slow crumpling
of this life for the sake
of all those sick children
who would be horrified
beyond the telling
if they ever saw you
torturing a living creature.
With eyes you wish
would not stare so.

The Birds

Daphne du Maurier's eco parable
of animals finally rebelling against human domination
was warped via Hitchcock's twisted mind
into a parable of failed human relationships.
Famously known for calling actors cattle,
and reportedly miffed that Tippi Hedren,
his blonde star, had rebuffed his advances,
the director herded her through scenes
involving the tying of live birds to her body.
They didn't want to peck at her
but he needed to make the pain real.

When I was growing up, this movie
was legendary among the neighborhood kids.
None of us had seen it but we all knew about it.
One boy claimed that the movie was awash in blood
with scene after scene of crazed birds
pecking out people's eyes, the body count
progressing steadily into the robust double figures.
The rest of us didn't quite believe him,
but we wanted to think such a film existed,
so we encouraged his descriptions
and embellished them with speculations of our own.
I saw the movie on late night television years later.
That shot where the camera
zooms into a man's bloody eye sockets
in three quick jump cuts,
holding the carnage for a split second,
is like a quiet piece of a disturbing dream.

The ending resolves nothing.
Thousands of the birds assemble
on roofs, fences, porch railings, and power lines,
like a vast choir tuning up for a reverent song,
while the humans get into their car and drive away.
Hedren gave up acting soon after this movie
and eventually opened a sanctuary for animals.
The rest of us remember that mechanical seagull
swooping down on her character
as she pilots her little boat across Bodega Bay.

It's a real place on the California coast,
north of San Francisco. Every time I look in the road atlas
and see the tiny dot next to those two words,
I remember the storm of birds flowing
down the chimney and filling up the living room,
the lives, of those unfortunate imagined people.

What a Friend Told Me About the Men in Her Family

Hunters only ask to hunt.
Men who hunt don't cheat
on their wives. They don't
look at other women or
go on benders and carouse
with their friends. Men who
hunt are good citizens and
they devote themselves to
their families. They pay their
bills and hold jobs and are
solid support to their children.
Men who hunt know that
taking a life is a sacred act.
They kill to feed those they
love and only ask for one thing:
to spend time in the woods,
alone, feeling the power of
the natural world. Men who
hunt are gone much of the time.
Their wives worry, at first, but
men who hunt inspire confidence.
Men who hunt don't know
any other way to live.

It's Like a Reflection of Life

the fishing net holds a flopping piece of food
still alive until the man who pulled it
out of the river clubs it twice
crushing its skull and bloodying its
scales and now a dead thing occupies
the space where a live creature once
pulled nourishment from the world
straining it through its gills and mouth
living on the pulse of the wet earth

The Power of Myth

We anticipated the centaur's
visitation with pleasure,
but soon discovered
centaurs piss everywhere,
trample everything,
and curse at everyone.
This behavior continued for weeks,
with citizens grumbling about
the boneheads who brought him
to our quiet town.
Eventually a drive-by shooting
left him bleeding in the street.
Many volunteers helped dig his grave.
His resting place remains unmarked.
Today people curse eloquently
if you ever mention his name.

The Pond on a Day Without Wind

the still surface
makes a twin
of each
floating duck

and holds
them all
upside down

with their beaks
breathing the
deep water

easy like
roots slithering
into the cool
clean ground

Elk

Through binoculars
the racks on the heads
of the elk herd
look like a suburb
of precariously balanced
houses of cards,
improbably constructed
and poised to crumple to the ground.
One head turns to face me,
antlers pivoting on a point of grace,
their owner perhaps noting
the bilateral branching
rooted in my eyes.

At his repose,
legs tucked under belly touching grass,
the elk's eyes
are too distant to read.
He comes from a mythic realm
where reindeer and shamans
live by eating magic.

He sees me watching him.
Through optic antlers
I scan side to side
in a slow motion mimic
of his head turns,
panning his nurtured tree
of fibrous tissue
wrapped in a soft bark,
rooted in the foreign soil
of his fertile skull.

Our Cat, Who Used to Bring Live Snakes Into the House

They were leaf-brown tubes of frenzy
twisting on white linoleum, our cat
placing her paw at their necks
stilling them for sure. We rescued
tangles of snakes from her
commanding limbs and put them
outside to hunt for small
creatures of their own. That
startling shiver of dry skin,
a bumpy memory now of how
our cat did not kill any of them,
and how we gave her away
so long ago I have to count
the years by recalling moving vans.
Those snakes she carried in,
they weren't exactly food, and now,
today, in a place thousands of
miles away, that cat, our cat,
I think, is very likely dead.

René Descartes Looked Through a Bull's Eyeball

and saw the world
upside down.
The bull wasn't seeing

much of anything
at that point.
Mr. D. spent a lot of time

trying to prove
God exists.
In the end, the best

he could do
was convince himself
of his own materiality.

It wasn't much,
but we have looked
through his eyes

and can speculate
it made him feel better
about the bull.

The Sad Vegetarian

There's a hoopla happening,
the din of fatal music filling the void.
A gathering of carnivores,
creatures stepping in an ancient rhythm.
The tuneful clicking of teeth and claws,
the eaters and the eaten
slow dancing to the churning beat
of an empty stomach,
with only a few left standing
when the lights go out.
They're sated and sleepy,
but fortified at the end
to dance another day
with another partner:
red visions of life as flesh.
It is the danger of it all,
the invigorating awful chance
that each tango is a possibility
for having to expose that neck
in a presentation of surrender.
Whispering so quiet
as to be inaudible.
The plea for swiftness
and the pulsing gasping rush,
there to brighten a last view
just before the darkness.

Canine Reminder

The dogs of my childhood:
potential energy on four legs,
coiled packages of teeth
and claws and menace.

Their noses taking my fear,
translating it into the knowledge
that I was not the alpha.
Could never be the alpha.

The first time someone looked at me
with fear: a child seeing an
unknown adult male, bearded,
too tall, potential menace
of grown up energy.

For a moment I was
the reluctant alpha male
smiling to dispel her fear.
Bared teeth like the growls
of dogs when they weighed
more than I did.

Yip Yip Yip

Coyote speaks
from beyond the hills
where all the voices
live together in a house
built by wind
and held together
by the mesh of
our imaginations.

We are ignited
on a path reaching
to the horizon's edge
where sound moves
into our muscles
and animates the
will to understand
the structure of howling.

Scavengers

They're bathing
in the pool

which evaporates
as you get

closer. You think
you're going to

crush them under
your steel belted

radials but they
fly to the sides

and wait as you
straddle the bloody

roadkill casting a
momentary flash of

shadow on its
denouement. In the

rearview mirror they
return to their

interrupted meal
like a reader picking

up the story at the
bookmarked page.

The Sound of Blue Jays at 6 a.m.

ripe flesh of strawberry
studded with seeds
and dappled by beak holes

you planted food for birds
and in the morning
listen to their thanks

An Ode to Moles

Master tunnelers scraping arteries
out of the earth, you are great
aerators of soil. Fresh heaps of dirt
like mushrooming mountain ranges
decorate lawns and tell the world:
a digger has been here and carved
a place for mole and mole kin to
live and make a society. Of sky
you know little. The sun is a distant
heat, and air, that thin nothing,
you know to leave to others, the
ones who swim through it on legs
paddling the roof of your world.
Wrapped in a dark embrace, you rest
after a day of crawling through the
endless network. You pull down carrots
we have planted, and chew, and sniff
subterranean aromas, redolent with the
silent memories of past mole generations.
Who once dug where you dig. Who once
made a home of humus in the cool inches.

Lunch Break

The seashore carpeted
by moist seaweed,
squishy where we step,
sending up an aroma
like fresh sushi.

Across the blue water,
a slab of earth
like a giant slice
of cake frosted with
bright green icing.

I avoid pressing my
heel on the remnants
of crustaceans, food for
seagulls, gliding above
us, waiting for dessert.

Calling Card

buzzed by a dark shape
in my peripheral vision
I look up to see a line of brown splashes
angling across the living room window

three fresh moist glyphs
that make me think of squashed bugs
or burst snowballs
that have been laced with mud

they may be the product
of bird terror and a last second veer
preventing a full speed head slam
into the glass pane separating me
from the world out there

at other times I have seen
feathers and blood stains
marking the glass
over a broken necked bird
on the deck below

and decide today's decorations
however unwelcome
are better than grieving
for the tiny life
wrung from those tiny bones
and bent feathers
and alien yellow eyes

Milk

Feed milk to
bacteria and
let it solidify:
call it cheese.
Put it on a
cracker, wash
it down with
some wine.

We like butter
but it's made
from stuff
that's meant
for calves.

Cows are machines
for turning grass
into cream
and yogurt.
Buttermilk, even.
Velvety fat
globules that
make you feel
like sleeping.

You'll find milk
in chocolate and
salad dressing.
Adult people
eating another
species's baby food.
Raiding the larder.
Not wanting
to grow up.

Last Rites for Roadkill

I know of those
who retrieve bits of the carcass:
quills for art pieces,
the flesh for stew or soup,
feathers to bless
some fleeting fantasy of flight.

Usually I register the remains
in my peripheral vision
and grimly drive on,
avoiding the vision of the former life
zipped open and spread out
like a sacrament on the pavement.

Once in Wyoming on interstate 80
the lanes were lumpy
with dead prairie dogs.
They had tried crossing the road,
following a migratory instinct,
and were crushed in their tracks.
Streaking fur disappeared
under the car. I pulled my foot
off the gas pedal but not in time.

The steering wheel
hiccupped a slight jump.
The car shuddered.
I opened my mouth in bewilderment.
The shock of killing
and the grief of loss
all in two round syllables:
oh no oh no oh no.

Menagerie

I carry the images
of animal eyes
that have locked with mine,
some for long cat seconds
others for brief deer moments.

The electricity,
latent in my body,
sparked a little
at each encounter,
the two of us
at opposite shores
of the separating gulf,
fear and wonder
defining our brief contact.

Visiting for a time,
then gliding away,
like magnetic norths
invoking a repulsive instinct
for the safe familiar.

Frying Eggs

The feathers
the beaks and wings
the yellow feet.
They are all
there in the
barnyard
of the pan
clucking
and congealing
holding the
perimeter
like the chickens
they might have been.

Cycle of Metamorphosis

the worms were frenzied green
writhing and plentiful as grass

a carpet of squishy fibers
our disgust a universal twitch

but then weeks later came
the moths tiling our windows

seeking the light on their
inward spiral and cocooning

us indoors where we waited
for their dirty brown wings

There's a Yellow Ladybug

There's a yellow ladybug
on the cupboard door of
Mary and Lloyd's house.
We never used to see
so many of them says Mary
and we don't know where
they come from but they are
everywhere this year.
The yellow ladybug crawls
near the handle and I tell Kim.
There's a yellow ladybug in the
kitchen, I say. And it's alive.

Comfort Zone

The bear was black
like a moving pit
opening in the green
underbrush just off
Wind River Road.
It flowed uphill
to dense foliage, not
wanting to see what
we looked like in
the safety of our car.
If it told stories
it might have a
good one about a
blue Honda trailing
a plume of dust
and stopping in
a place where any
bear could see it
was smaller than
the car and had to
run away for safety.
My heart's easy flutter
was a steady presence
in my chest as I
watched the bear
and knew one thing:
without this garment
made of steel and
glass I would feel
the rattle of my
chest muscle. It
would want to
move, escape, even
fly and would not
necessarily wait for
me, reluctant and
confused traveling
companion.

Location Location Location

Hold a white feather in your hand.
Raise it to the sky.
Let it sail on a puff of your breath.
Watch it fall, curved side down,
to a soft landing on the grass.

Stand in a flock of barn swallows.
Raise your feather to the sky.
Tilt your head and blow.
Swallows swoop and swirl around you
in swift rustling arcs
until one or two seconds later
your offering is snatched from the air
safely lodged in a swallow's beak
and disappears with its owner into a nearby nest
accompanied by a throaty liquid note of thanks
and you
are left
with a smile, curved side down,
looking for another feather.

Juncos

are inadvertent
master musicians

spilling sunflower
seeds from the bird

feeder to the grass
below, conducting

a future chorus of
singing yellow petals.

Sanderling Flight, Sanderling Walk

Sanderlings, their legs
scissoring the surf.
They stop,
beaks pivot forward,
tasting the sea.

The flock of them
an ad hoc creature
made of bird cells.
Their voices are muted
in the aquamarine sheen.

They gather their shape
and rise,
skimming over waves,
stitching a sky quilt
with their invisible thread.

Final Journey

You're gasping in this strange realm.
It's an odd thin water enveloping you.
Your flanks embedded by talons.
Residual drops from your receding home
slide off your scales and punctuate
a line stretching to the landscape below.
Did you wonder about this place, ever?
Did you look up and long for a visit
to the world on the other side? Did
you know death flourished there,
in the form of a raptor trolling for
takeout? Your roof now is a wavy mat
of feathers, protecting and concealing your
dispatcher's belly, soon to be your resting
place. An unexpected mercy begins to
cloud your eyes and obscure your senses.
Robustly muscled wings lift you with
rhythmic pulsing pumping strokes.
You're flying, vertigo the last sensation
throbbing through your protein-rich flesh.

Lost and Found

The guy in town
who spends his days
collecting cans and bottles
hands me his green plastic
garbage bag like it's
a holy treasure.
He grins and says
you lost these
over by the foot bridge
above Rock Creek.

I have stood on that bridge
and watched salmon
swim against the hard current
but what could I have
left there? Thank you
I say and upend the bag.
Words tumble out
onto the ground.

I cannot speak.
The light of the sun
glints off the edges
of all those consonants
and the wind howls
through the vowels.

Missing Fingers

I never believed those stories
of people finding finger tips
complete with the untrimmed dirty nail
in a mound of supermarket hamburger.
They seemed too calculated
to turn the stomachs
of unprepared listeners.
The people I've known
who have lost fingers
in accidents with machinery
or through careless use of sharp tools
have been too considerate of body parts
to upset those of others
by carelessly leaving
their appendage
at the scene of the mishap.

The songwriter
who played the guitar for me
strumming flawless chords
despite a gap
where his ring finger should have been
was too squeamish
to slaughter his own livestock.
On winter nights
he brought lambs
in from the cold
where they could warm up
next to his wood stove.
He sat petting them
wool curling
around his four
remaining digits.

An Insomniac's Machinations

Early afternoon
by Catherine Creek:

brown bat body
suspended on black

wings. Lost in the
warm sun and bare

trees looking for
its disturbed nest

maybe. The cave
misplaced. Its

senses too small
for all this

light. It veers
toward me,

rabidly searching
for something

familiar. Finding
a way to the rocks.

I watch it closely.
It doesn't know

I'm hoping for
its imminent

suspension of this
unnatural dream.

Evolutionary Thoughts

I heard on the radio today
that four million years ago
certain Antarctic fish
transformed some of their own
digestive enzymes
into antifreeze compounds
that today keeps their descendants
from becoming floating blocks of ice
at the southern extreme of the planet.

To be the researcher
who discovered this mutation
tumbling across the years of deep time
must be like witnessing
the course of a meandering ant
gathering the stuff of sustenance
in a field of grass
and tripping it back
to the mass of her writhing siblings
boiling up from her home mound.

The pulse of life
there in the surges and waves
of an ant colony
and silently echoed
in a fish's bloodstream
are just the end of a process
initiated by mysterious means
at an unimaginable genesis
that some of us
with characteristic hubris
believe we can understand.

In Ancient Times We
Crawled Around On
Our Bellies and Did
Not Sprout Arms and
Legs Until the Odd
and Mysterious Ways
of Natural Selection
Deemed it Feasible
for Us to Walk on
Our Feet and Pick
Up Things and Throw
Them at Each Other

The hand contains too
many bones to count, and all
of them can be broken.

Unnatural Selection

Extracted from The Origin of Species *by Charles Darwin.*

Such variability
is simply due
to our domestic production.
The many foxes,
inhabiting different quarters of the world,
briefly give them one definition.
None has yet satisfied
all naturalists.
The full number of a tree
is the store of nutriment
laid up within the seeds
of many plants
at a corresponding age.
These experiments
were published elsewhere.
The number of the native
genera and species.
In the same way,
for instance,
the English race-horse
has adapted males
for the greatest number of offspring.
Some of these cannot possibly
be here introduced.
It is the steady accumulation
through natural selection.
For species,
the same rule
will probably apply to both.
Animals exist
having every intermediate grade.
I can, indeed, hardly doubt
that all vertebrate animals
will see nearly similar hooks
on many trees.
And on the doors
in the morning and evening.

Deep Time

The cows in their meadow
staring us down
on the safe side of the fence
must know.
They accumulate flies
in a dense buzz of black
hovering on their lips and ears.
Uncaring and perfectly made
for this grass living
they are the repeated reflection
of history's sculpting.
Beings like us have made
cows into what they would not
otherwise have been.
But our purposely made
alternate history
does not quell the fear
of what they once were
or the thought
of how far their eyes
have traveled.

Being Content With Who You Are

Coffee klatch of seals
sunning and visiting
on a barnacled rock,
a moat of salt water
ringing their perch.

I stand on the still shore
safe from their animation,
waves undulating their blubber
in rising and lowering tides.
They're little packets of ocean,

flopped up on dry rock,
and they move about in rocking
motions, watching me
watching them repeat the lives
of endless seas always eroding.

Not Much of a Protector

We can all imagine a dancing
path through falling raindrops.

Years ago, during a break from work
at the mill, moon moths circled

the ground at my feet, spinning
endless spirals in the dust.

It was as though their wings
were too big, the weight of life

keeping them from flight. I
watched them, puzzled, amused.

One of my co-workers leaned against
the wall beside me, blowing smoke

into the air. The boss had just
chewed him out for sitting down

on the job and I knew he hated
the endless stream of ore

torn from underground. Wordlessly,
he pushed his shovel's blade

through the fat body of a turning moth,
dividing it into two unmoving nubs.

The wings, perversely, were unharmed,
green and large like spring fields.

I was quiet as he stared silently,
then turned with smooth grace from his

killing and looked across the hill
to black clouds just visible over

the horizon. Rain's coming, he said.
Soon spatters of water exploded

on his boots and tossed up tiny
bursts of dust beside the dead moth.

Suddenly Dangerous

The killdeer emits short sharp cries
and runs swiftly on scissoring legs.

I see its profile across the meadow,
needle beak thrust angling to the sky,

repeating that single note alarm,
halting my afternoon stroll.

Somewhere close by is a clutch of eggs
in a nest hidden from my clumsy foot.

I imagine I see nests all around me
camouflaged on the muddy ground

sheltering embryonic killdeer,
unseen hearts pulsing in my still ears.

Spring Morning After the Last Snow has Melted

My lawn mower
is a killing machine
shredding grass
mice snakes frogs.

Up ahead the
green crop beckons
uneven and wild
never suspecting.

Behind me
the birds come
looking for
bloody meals

in the buzz
cut expanse.
And the moles.
Their mounds

dusty and heaped
up into an
archipelago
of crumbly peaks.

I cut around
them like
a climber stuck
in the foothills.

Bigfoot

In his last few years
Datus took oxygen through a plastic tube
from a portable tank
he pushed around on big black wheels.
He'd tell stories of the two times
he met Bigfoot in the woods
and how on both occasions
she made advances toward him
that he understood to be
of a distinctly provocative nature.
Perhaps they were the misguided impulses
of a lonely creature missing her true mate.
Datus said he didn't stick around
long enough to find out.
But he did get a good enough
look at her to spend a lot of time
drawing her portrait from memory
and making photocopies of her likeness
at the library's copy machine.
He would emit growling sounds
from deep in his throat
as he pushed the print button repeatedly.
An earthy aroma drifted up
from his clothes as he worked
and his hair was wild and uncombed.
His beard grew unimpeded
by conventional grooming standards
and in his milky eyes
it was just possible
to see a hint of longing and regret
at not having seen his lady
since those first meetings
five decades ago.

Perfectionism

I guess psychologists call it
overcompensation for perceived lacks,
this need to be right.

Or is it that the instinct to belong
makes me want to be
as competent as a machine?

Look at the ants
pushing grains of millet
off the cliff edge of a flat rock.
Their actions are unmarred
by doubts about their abilities
or questions about their purpose.
They accumulate a string
of tiny irregular globes
strung out at the rock base
like lumpy yellow pearls
arranged in a perfect jagged line.

Look at the work of ants
who strive to be nothing
other than ants:
leg tips click click clicking
under their oversized burden
securing their hold on what's real.

Rudderless in Bandon

thousands of jellyfish
blue with white sails
tessellating the beach

marooned in the sun
catching an easterly
and going nowhere

Still Healthy

My friend came over
looking for the eggs
he had left with me
last week. "They're in
the laundry room," I
said, recalling how
I had forgotten them
only seven days ago.

"I don't think they
can be any good now,"
I said. "I'm sorry. I
don't know where my
head is at these days."

"It's ok," he said. We
went to the laundry
room where the yellow
chicks had hatched
and were standing on
the dryer. A dozen of
them looking back at
us, wanting to be fed.

"These eggs look fine
to me," said my friend.

Shadows Make the Ground More Real

The crow's dark twin
is a flattened gliding
patch, form-fitting,
flowing over
grass and pebbles.

But you know the dim
apparitions we call
ghosts: they move like
shadows and have lost
a dimension like some

people lose a tooth.
They try to push it
back in with the edge
of their tongue pressed
against the wet slot.

Alzheimer's

Three hundred thousand million
days ago
a creature died.

And a slab of rock
kept its memory embedded
in brittle wrinkled folds
for a billion years,

until a fossil hunter
chipped away the image
of the creature

and the rock
reached into the void repeatedly.
But found nothing.

Eventually the rock forgot
there was ever anything there
and stopped reaching.

Genealogy

One of my ancestors
was the kind of insect
that eats anything
even its own children.

One of my ancestors
gave birth to a sterile
baby who therefore never
extended his branch
of the family tree.

One of my ancestors
lived in the sea and
was constantly wary
of attacks from other
ocean creatures.

One of my ancestors
started a family of
five children then left
them all one day
and spent the rest of
her years atop a cold
and barren mountain.

One of my ancestors
remembered a time when
the Earth had no
multicelled creatures.

One of my ancestors
looked just like
the oak tree rooted
at the corner a block
away from my house.

One of my ancestors
was a cheetah
who had to kill

an antelope every week
just to survive
another seven days.

One of my ancestors
was a snake who crawled
on the ground and ate
her meals whole.

One of my ancestors
had wings made of feathers
but dreamed of building
houses out of stone.

One of my ancestors
was killed when lava
from a volcano turned
him into a fossil
that a geologist found
ten million years later
and discarded as being
too ordinary.

One of my ancestors
killed many people
and was finally killed
himself when he fell
from a mountain path
to a field of rocks
a thousand feet below.

One of my ancestors
discovered religion
and used it to make
other people feel
as though they could
not live in this world.

One of my ancestors

flew to the moon
before anyone knew
what the moon was
but did not tell
anyone because she
thought the moon was
better off without
anymore visitors.

One of my ancestors
could foretell the future
but chose not to do so
as the knowledge only
made him so terrified
of life he would remain
in bed for weeks at a time.

One of my ancestors
lived her last few years
as a tattoo on a biker's
upper arm right next
to the heart with
the sword through it.

One of my ancestors
was so small he
lived in the arteries
of a hummingbird.

One of my ancestors
was harpooned by a
whaling ship but lived
to tell the story
many times.

One of my ancestors
was crushed by
a falling meteorite.

One of my ancestors
did not speak
for sixty years
then said good bye
and died an hour later.

One of my ancestors
ate only a certain
kind of leaf that she
found by following
the flight paths of
birds who nested
only in those
kinds of trees.

One of my ancestors
was a peach who
lived in the middle
part of an old
limb on a worn peach tree.

One of my ancestors
spoke to rocks
who spoke back to her.

One of my ancestors
emerged from the sun
and spent a million years
wandering the solar system
until she decided
to settle down here on Earth.

One of my ancestors
was a crab who could
never get enough
of the salt spray
splashing his shell.

One of my ancestors

sulked whenever it
looked as though he
was about to be served
a helping of broccoli.

One of my ancestors
was a centaur who
loved women and horses
but would never allow
any of them to love him.

One of my ancestors
was allergic to bee stings
and never ate honey.

One of my ancestors
grew a rack of antlers
every year and no one
not even the other bucks
ever said a word about it.

One of my ancestors
swam the length
of the Mississippi
River upstream.

One of my ancestors
was born in a garbage dump
and spent all her days
there and could not think
of a better way to live.

One of my ancestors
stole a horse and was hung
by his angry fellow citizens.

One of my ancestors
regularly drank six beers
a day and smoked two packs

of cigarettes but would
not drive because it was
too dangerous.

One of my ancestors
took five years out of his life
to count the grains of sand
on the beach behind his house.

One of my ancestors
was the voice
for a famous cartoon character
no one remembers anymore.

One of my ancestors
built a ship
to bring invaders
from one part of the world
to destroy the people
in another part of the world.

One of my ancestors
was the first creature
to lie to another creature.

One of my ancestors
had a long tail
that she liked to curl
around the branches of trees
from where she would drop
fruit on creatures passing
beneath her and laugh
until her tail uncurled
and she fell on her head
and forgot who or what
or where she was.

The Index to the Bestiary of Extinct Species

Many of the animals have
names I don't recognize.
When I turn to the indicated
pages I find descriptions of
creatures written like the
entries in a high school yearbook
before it becomes known
which ones were really
the most likely to succeed.

Plato's Menagerie

The ideal zoo
would be like
a certain theologian's
concept of hell:
it exists
but it's empty.

Dramatis Personae

ant • 79, 89
antelope • 95
bacteria • 65
badger • 38
barnacle • 83
bat • 78
bear • 12, 30, 71
bee • 24, 40, 98
Bigfoot • 88
bird • 14, 22, 35, 41, 48, 64, 87, 97
blackbird • 43
blue jay • 61
bull • 56
butterfly • 21
cat • 55
centaur • 52, 98
cheetah • 94
chicken • 68, 91
chipmunk • 16
cow • 25, 48, 65, 82
coyote • 59
crab • 97
crow • 34, 46, 92
crustacean • 63
dog • 18, 22, 33, 58
dragonfly • 12
duck • 53
elk • 54
fish • 22, 37, 51, 79
flea • 24
fly • 26, 82
fox • 81
frog • 87
goose • 38
grasshopper • 45
great blue heron • 20
grub • 44

horse • 81, 98
hummingbird • 96
insect • 22, 94
jellyfish • 90
junco • 73
killdeer • 86
ladybug • 70
lamb • 77
leopard • 11
mole • 62, 87
moth • 69, 84
mouse • 16, 31, 41, 87
osprey • 37
owl • 16
paramecium • 27
peacock • 28
pigeon • 36
prairie dog • 66
red-winged blackbird • 19
raccoon • 42
raven • 13
reindeer • 32
salmon • 12, 30, 37, 76
sanderling • 74
seagull • 48, 63
seal • 83
snake • 15, 23, 28, 55, 95
spider • 24, 41
starling • 39
swallow • 39, 72
turtle • 12, 25
whale • 96
wolverine • 38
woodpecker • 44
worm • 69

Acknowledgements

The poems in *Animal Life* are previously unpublished, except as noted here:

"Bigfoot" originally appeared online in *The Endicott Studio Journal of Mythic Arts*, (http://www.endicott-studio.com/jMA04Summer/chBigFoot.html) Summer 2004.

"Dinner and Dancing" originally appeared in *Rosebud*, #25, 2002.

"A Disturbance in the Field" originally appeared in *Snowy Egret*, Spring 2001, vol. 64, #1.

"Evidence" originally appeared in *Midwest Poetry Review*, April 2001.

"Final Journey" originally appeared in *Midwest Poetry Review*, April 2001.

"Missing Fingers" originally appeared in *4th Street*, May/June 2003.

"On Learning That Owls Hunt by Starlight" originally appeared in *Rockford Review*, Winter 2002, vol. XXI, #1.

"Plato's Menagerie" originally appeared in *EDGZ* #4, Summer/Fall 2002.

"The Power of Myth" originally appeared in *Asimov's SF*, June 2003.

"Reindeer Presence" originally appeared online in *The Endicott Studio Journal of Mythic Arts*, (http://www.endicott-studio.com/jMA04Winter) Winter 2004.

"She's Eve: A Walking Poem" originally appeared in *Snake Nation Review* #16, 2003.

"What a Friend Told Me About the Men in Her Family" originally appeared in *4th Street*, July/August 2002.

"When I Was" originally appeared online in *The Endicott Studio Journal of Mythic Arts*, (http://www.endicott-studio.com/jMA03Autumn) Autumn 2003.

About the Author

Mario Milosevic lives with his wife, novelist Kim Antieau, in Bigfoot country in Washington State on the banks of the Columbia River, where he works at a small town library. His poems have appeared in many print and online journals, and in the anthology *Poets Against the War*. A companion volue, *Fantasy Life*, is also available.

www.ingramcontent.com/pod-product-compliance
Lightning Source LLC
Chambersburg PA
CBHW030100100526
44591CB00008B/209